D0529691

Wild Flamingos

written and photo-illustrated by Bruce McMillan

Houghton Mifflin Company
Boston 1997

For those who work to protect flamingo habitats

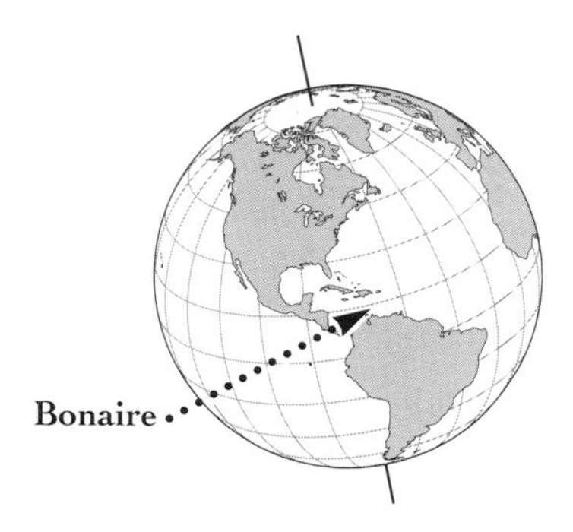

Wild Flamingos was photographed in March 1995 on the south Caribbean island of Bonaire, Netherlands Antilles. It was shot using a Nikon F4/MF23 with 24, 85, 105 micro, 180, 300, and 600 mm lenses. A polarizing filter was often used when shooting in full sunlight. The 35 mm film, Kodachrome 64, was processed by Kodak at Fair Lawn, New Jersey.

This book was made possible through the generous help and support of the Tourism Corporation of Bonaire, Kaya Simon Bolivar #12, Kralendijk, Bonaire, Netherlands Antilles (NA); Ronnie Pieters, director, Gabrielle Nahr, Lorna Wanga, and Rolando Sint Yago; Stinapa, the Bonaire National Parks Foundation, Roberto Hensen, chairman; Akzo Nobel Salt Company, Jan Gielen, plant manager; Avis Car Rental, Denise Simon; Richard's, Richard F. Beady; and Frater Candidas.

For information about this and other Houghton Mifflin trade and reference books and multimedia products, visit The Bookstore at Houghton Mifflin on the World Wide Web at http://www/hmco.com/trade/.

Walter Lorraine  Books

Library of Congress Cataloging-in-Publication Data

McMillan, Bruce.
Wild flamingos / written and photo-illustrated by Bruce McMillan. p. cm.
Includes bibliographical references and index.
Summary: A photo essay describing the physical characteristics, natural habitat, and behavior of the flamingos of Bonaire, Netherlands Antilles.
ISBN 0-395-84545-9
1. Greater flamingo—Bonaire—Juvenile literature. [1. Greater flamingo. 2. Flamingos.]
I. Title
QL696.C56M38 1997
598.3'5—dc21 97-1521
CIP AC

Printed in Singapore TWP 10 9 8 7 6 5 4 3 2 1

Design and typesetting by Bruce McMillan.
The text is set in 14-point Cochin.

*"There are larger birds than the flamingo,
and birds with more brilliant plumage,
but no other large bird is so brightly colored
and no other brightly colored bird is so large."*

—Dr. Frank Michler Chapman, 1908
Curator of Ornithology,
American Museum of Natural History

Spring
Bonaire, Netherlands Antilles

A young flamingo walks among the flock. It is easily seen because it hasn't grown its bright orange-red feathers yet. Like the adults, it walks in a lake, not in the nearby ocean. Wind may ripple the lake, but there is no overpowering surf.

This is a salina—a lake below sea level that is filled with salt water from the sea. It rarely rains, so fresh water doesn't dilute it. As the water evaporates, the salina becomes saltier and saltier. The least salty part is the inlet where the ocean flows in. This is where the flamingos come to splash and bathe.

Thousands of greater flamingos, the largest of all the flamingo species, live free in salinas on the small Caribbean island of Bonaire. It is only fifty miles north of Venezuela. Although the island is desert-like, there is food for the flamingos in the briny (salty) water. It is this food that makes the birds the most colorful flamingos in the world.

While one flamingo pauses, another sticks its head underwater to feed on tiny animals. It eats some small shellfish. Flamingos at the other end of the island eat immature brine flies—both free-swimming larvae and the intermediate chrysalid stage, which are attached to rocks on the bottom. All of these little animals eat aquatic plants and bacteria that contain the same chemicals that make carrots orange. The effect of these chemicals is to give the flamingo a beautiful, bright orange-red color. If this food chain stops, and a flamingo eats only food without these chemicals, its bright colors fade back to gray and white, the colors of its youth.

The water is deeper in the salinas at the northern end of the island. One flamingo, like all the others in the flock, uses its long neck to look for immature flies. Flamingos always eat with their heads upside down. The top bill is hinged and moves up and down like a person's lower jaw.

All around the salinas, spiny candle and prickly pear cactuses grow. Standing in water thirty inches deep, a flamingo sticks its neck straight down. Another flamingo swims to a different part of the salina to feed in deeper water. With its outstretched neck, and webbed feet splashing for balance, this flamingo pushes its head down as far as it can go.

Each flamingo filter-feeds, using its tongue as a piston to pump water through tiny filter-like teeth that line the inside of the bill. It's an unusual way to eat—like a baleen whale.

Flamingos are very social. They like to be together, even if they are just standing around. Though they like the company of the flock, they don't like others to get too close. The space within a neck's reach they consider their own.

One flamingo gets too close to another. Feathers ruffle. Necks wave. Bills are ready to nip. They honk at each other. The intruder backs off. Everyone goes back to eating—until one wanders too close again.

Hungry flamingos skim their bills just beneath the water, feeding on the immature brine flies. One walks along the shore, swinging its head like a pendulum while sucking in swarms of adult brine flies. The insects are small, and a flamingo spends half of its entire day just eating. It eats up to a million tiny insects in a month.

As a walking flamingo feeds, it leaves behind a footprint in the mud at the water's edge. Super-salty water fills the webbed imprint and evaporates in the hot sun, leaving a salt print.

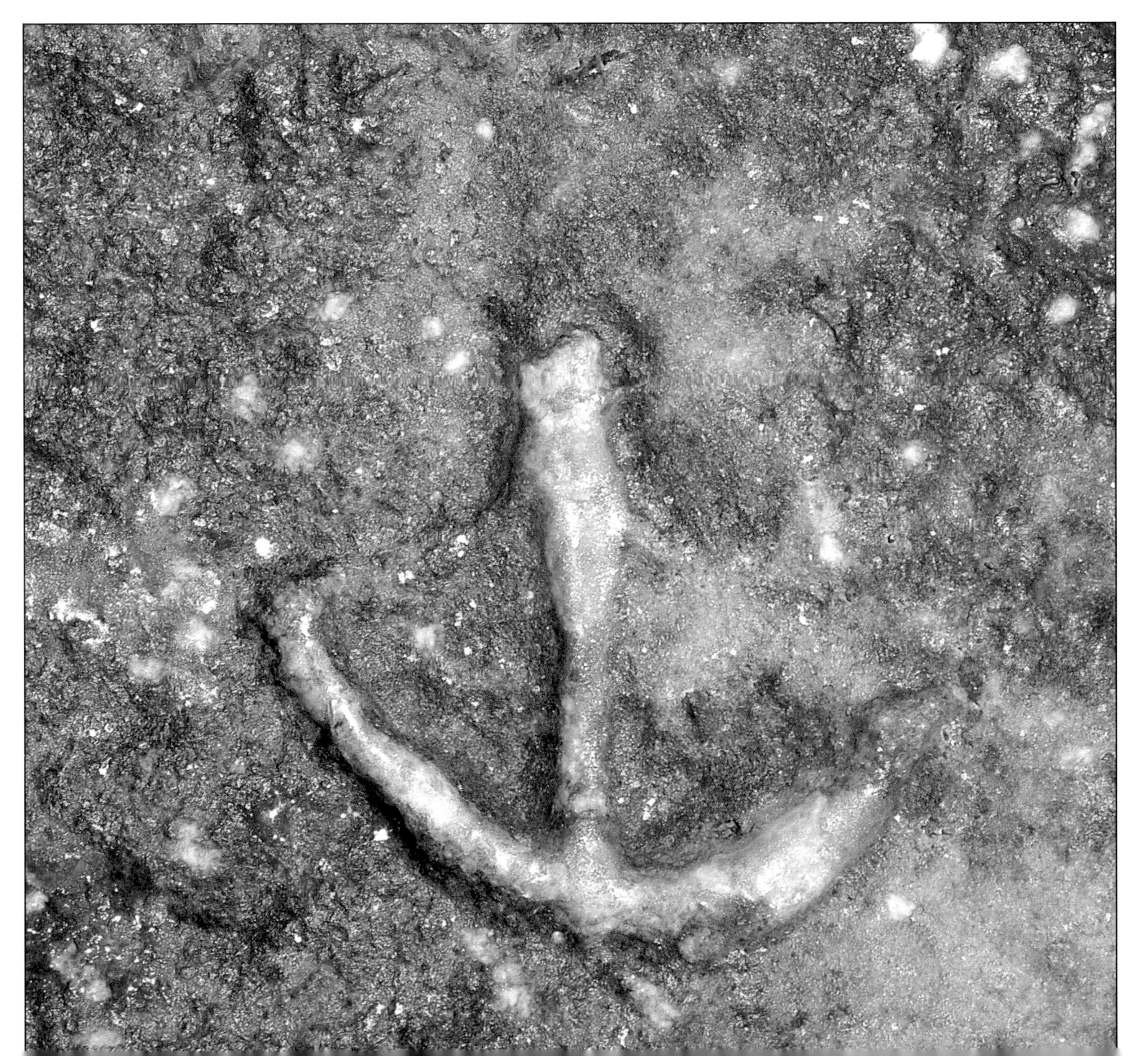

A flamingo looks around. Its yellow eyes face out to the sides, each with its own wide panoramic view. It is alert, even though there are no wild predators here. But the flamingos are always wary and on the lookout for anything unusual or for people approaching.

One of the flock is alarmed by something. It stretches its neck as high as it can and turns its head from side to side, checking all around. The others start checking too. Necks stretch high and heads turn, swiveling back and forth. The birds look all around. Nothing. False alarm.

False alarm or not, they decide to move to another part of the salina. The parade of long-legged birds begins. These are the tallest of all the wading birds. They honk as they walk along.

Once settled, some flamingos scratch. Others twist their necks and lay their heads on their backs to rest. The flamingos' bodies are high above the water. They stand on one leg and hold the other leg folded up beneath them. Even while resting on one leg, they have a good sense of balance.

One flamingo with its head on its back looks as if it is sleeping, but it isn't. It's preening, picking out worn feathers and making space for new ones to grow. Other flamingos are doing the same thing, twisting their necks to preen their whole bodies. They are picking and smoothing their feathers while laying them flat. Old feathers fall and float away. The drifting feathers are blown across the water and lost in bubbles of salt foam at the edge of the salina.

The sun beats down, and the trade winds blow. The sun and winds keep the temperature almost constant all year long, at eighty-one degrees Fahrenheit.

A flamingo stretches its neck to fluff all of its feathers. At the same time it shakes drops of water from its bill. Each drop is even saltier than the salina water it falls into. With no fresh water to drink, the flamingo drinks salt water and swallows some with its food. Its body removes the salt, leaving behind fresh water. It does this with a gland in its head that concentrates the salt, producing a small amount of super-salty water. Droplets of it flow from the gland and drip down its bill.

As another flamingo stretches its wings, its long black flight feathers appear. All this preening is in preparation for flight. Now the flamingos are ready to fly.

It is late afternoon. One flamingo starts walking slowly. Others walk along with it. They all walk faster and faster. They unfold their wings. They run, flapping their widespread wings. They seem to run on top of the water, flailing their webbed feet back and forth as they gain speed. They are aloft.

Only birds are allowed to fly on the northern and southern parts of Bonaire. The airspace above two thirds of this island, the areas where the flamingos live, is off-limits to planes. This is where the flamingos feed and raise their young, undisturbed by people.

But there is not enough food for all the flamingos at this time of year. It is spring. There are young ones to be fed. A flamingo heads south in search of more food. Flying at thirty miles per hour, it departs for the two-hour flight to Venezuela. With its neck stretched forward and long legs trailing behind, it looks like a flying stick with wings.

Venezuela is not a good place to nest and raise chicks, but it is a good place to find more food. This flamingo needs extra food because it has a young chick to feed on Bonaire. And so it will return tomorrow.

It is morning, and the flamingos are fully fed. The lead flamingo is returning home, on course, to its chick. Cone-shaped mud nests dot the nesting area of the salina. The downy gray chick is waiting, along with all the others. It is safe. People are never allowed to enter this area.

The returning parent lands. Only the flamingos are close enough to see it drip a dinner of red, fat-rich "crop milk" onto its bill and into the chick's open mouth. The "milk," made in glands that line the parent's throat, contains red and white blood cells. The parent who has been nesting leaves to feed and make another meal for the chick.

Nearby, older chicks stand together, making a long, gray, fluffy line. Adult flamingos stand guard. The weeks-old chicks are safe here in the middle of the shallow salina. All day they stand in the glaring hot sun, sometimes in the shade of their parents, waiting to be fed, waiting to grow up.

A young flamingo walks among the flock. Someday it will join the adults on their feeding trips. Tonight, it stays here. On this island it will grow into an adult and raise its chicks. It is safe on Bonaire because the people share the island with the flamingos.